I0425171

MAGAZINE MAN

A Slave to the Sale

Author: George C. Valentine
Editor: Chris Clanton
ISBN: 978-1456414023
Genre: Autobiography, Inspirational Non Fiction, Christian
Valentine Publishing
Copyright @ 2010 magazineman

Literary Agent: Diana Flegal
Hart line Literary Agency
123 Queenston Drive
Pittsburgh, PA 15235
412.915.1790
Email: diana@hartlineliterary.com

Table of Contents

Ephesians 5:11-14; and have no fellowship with the unfruitful works of darkness, but rather reprove them. For it is a shame even to speak of those things which are done in secret. But all things that are reproved are made manifest by the light: for whatsoever doth make manifest light. Wherefore he saith, Awake thou that sleepiest, and arise from the dead, and Christ shall give thee light.

Chapter One

Fun in the Sun

Ephesians 6:12; For we do not battle against flesh and blood, but against the rulers, against the principalities, and the authorities of the darkness of this age.

Here's my story:

It was like any other day in Pittsburgh PA; my brother Donnie and our friend Rick all set around listening to an ad on a radio station that was very popular back in 1991. We hardly paid attention to the station at all until an energetic voice came on offering a chance of a lifetime. The ad would later change our lives forever. I doubt I could ever forget what the ad said, "Wanted eighteen to twenty three year old guys and girls. Will travel to California to have fun in the sun and make lots of money! Participants must be energetic and outgoing. Call Ms. Crane for your interview today. Don't miss this once in a lifetime opportunity; travel arrangement will be free..." The ad was very compelling and both Rick and my brother called the number and had their follow up interviews quickly as planned at the Hyatt, a real nice hotel here in Pittsburgh.

I found myself equally as compelled by the promise of money and 'fun' my young mind raced with the possibility of getting out of this back water town I had grown up in. Growing up had not been easy my mother died when I was ten she died right in front of me and my brother with her eyes open the last thing she said was "I love you". I loved my mother and she loved me but she had her fair share of issues. She was in and out of mental hospitals they say she had eupepsy. On top of that she and my dad were both alcoholics and very physically abusive to me and my brother. My dad was a steel worker.

I can still remember how he would go to work and come back just to get drink and beat on my mother and us kids. It was terrible and the death of my mother just made things worse. After her death my dad shipped me out to my aunts and house in South Park. It was still hard for me all I could think about was my mother's death. When I turned 15 a relative had almost killed me so my dad took me back. I stayed with him for almost a year. That was until my dad found out that I skipped 67 days of school. He beat me with a small T.V. he got me for Christmas, so I moved in with my brother and started drinking and getting high.

Now this ad offered another way out I had just turned eighteen and the offer looked like a perfect opportunity for me. Rick and Donnie came back all excited and told me they were both able to get the job. They were both more interested in the young woman who had hired them however; she was apparently a very beautiful woman. They said that they were leaving for California in three days and encouraged me to sign up as well. The thought of escape and starting anew was all too good for me and I quickly gave Ms. Crane a call. She told me to come down for an interview first thing in the morning. I was bustling with excitement the next day when I came down for the interview.

The hotel was huge and I quickly discovered that the interview was to take place in the penthouse, and to say I was excited before was an understatement, now I wanted to burst. As I walked down the hall I found four other people were already lined up for an interview before me. I was so nervous I didn't know what to do with myself I wanted to get the job like my brother and Rick had. I only had to wait fifteen minutes but it felt more like an eternity before she finally called me in.

I walked into the room slowly and found Ms. Crane waiting for me. To say she was beautiful was an understatement. She was the most beautiful woman I had ever seen. She had long blonde hair and piercing blue eyes that locked me in her gaze. She wore a very short skirt and half her chest seemed to come out of the front of it. She gave me a small knowing smile and I felt my cheeks burn just slightly. She told me to sit wherever I would like and the interview started. It was hard to concentrate during the interview and it was hard to take my eyes off the beautiful half naked beauty before me. Two times she even dropped here pencil during the interview which I have very little doubt was done on purpose.

Her job I would later find out was to subdue young

men into the job and make it sound worthwhile which she did. The job would be relatively easy I would be selling cleaning products. She looked over my application and said I would be perfect for the job. To sum up the interview she showed me a photo album of beautiful young men and woman all having fun at the beach and at parks. I was hooked and told her I could start as soon as possible.

She said that she wanted me to call here in the next few days or so and she would tell me when to get on the bus to California. Naturally I said ok and went back home. My brother and Rick were already partying over there new job and when I told them I also got the job they quickly helped me celebrate it. I found out that they would both be leaving in the morning and I figured I would as well. But when I called Ms. Crane the next day she informed me that I would not be leaving for another two days. I was a little disappointed but I got on the bus two days later dropped off by my dad at the local greyhound station. My dad gave me forty bucks and wished me good luck. I was still a little scared I had never been out of Pittsburgh before but my excitement drove me on.

The ticket I had sad that I would be in Santa Ana California in three-in-a-half days. Unfortunately the trip took over five and I ran out of money the first two. And on the second day someone stole my last five dollars while I was asleep. The trip was already not going very well and after nearly a day without food I bummed some money off of someone on the bus I didn't know. I felt more than a little awkward but after hours of not eating I felt I had no choice. Most of the people on the bus were crazy drinking and passing out drugs I had ever seen before. The bus stunk like urine and dirty feet and was the worst five days of my life up to that point if only I had the since to see that it was just the beginning of the worst moments of my life.

It was two thirty in the morning five days after we left when the eternal bus ride from hell finally ended as we pulled up into the bus station. We quickly filed off the bus and once again I felt a little awkward being the only white kid out of the fifty plus that was getting off of the bus. There were gang members and drug dealers everywhere and I was scared out of my wits. I reached the nearest phone I could find and called Ms. Crane with the number she had given me and to my horror there was no answer! I called the number five times and waited for almost two hours before I got fed up and called a cab. At least she gave me the name of the hotel I would be staying at. I had no money and had to barter with the cab driver with a camera I had for him to take me to the Radisson in Newport Beach.

I was furious that no one had come to pick me up but at least the ride only took fifteen minutes. If I had any brains in my I would have turned back but I was young. When I stepped out before the hotel I was stunned at how huge it was, it towered about twenty five stories over the streets below. My anger was quickly forgotten as I figured that if I was going to stay in a hotel that big then what I had to gripe about. I walked into the front desk area which was bigger than the house I grew up in. I walked up to the front desk and caught the attention of the man behind the counter.

I asked for Todd's room, which had been the name that Ms. Crane had given me before I left. The man behind the counter called up to the room and a few minutes later Todd came out of the elevator. I instantly hated the man as he begrudgingly looked over at me and called me a few choice words before shuffling me after him after he told me to grab my things. Dragging my stuff after him I asked him if he knew where my brother was and he just grunted at me saying that he was asleep. When I asked if I could stay in the same room as my brother he shook his head and told me that I would be staying with him in his *training room.* There were three others in the room besides me and only two double size beds. Todd explained with a small smirk that I would be allowed my own bed for my first three days after that it would go by who could bring in the most business. The two who brought in the most sails would have the beds the two who brought in the least got to sleep on the floor!

I was so tired and dirty from being on the bus for five days that I hardly cared. I just took a shower and went to bed. At seven Todd woke me up shouting for me to get in the shower and not to back talk. I didn't argue. When I got out he told me that there was a meeting for all agents in room 1201 he told me that I better not be late or I would regret it. Still wondering about my brother and Rick I went to the room for the meeting and found them already there. I didn't have a chance to talk with them though because there was about fifteen hot girls that had stole my interest. A guy named Chris burst through the door a short time later everyone broke into cheers clapping the man on as he came through the door. Not knowing what else to do I did the same. He looked like Fabio from those entire comical, tall tan and handsome. He had a lot of flashy jewelry and a wallet full of cash. The first thing that Chris did was taking out a wad of cash and began passing out yesterday's bonuses.

Chris handed out over two hundred dollars between four people. He then had people pass out sales manuals and Todd quickly took me aside and started teaching me the sale pitches. They were broken into two teams the boys' teams and the girls' team. The girls sold magazines and the guys were to sell cleaning supply. After about thirty minutes the owner of the company Bobby Unger showed up and wow! The man was about six four about two hundred and seventy five pounds. He had jewelry hanging all over him and a Rolex made up of diamonds I later found out was worth over twenty five thousand dollars. The man was by all means intimidating. He was rich and big and he knew it. All the girls ran up to him to get there *'bonus'* money!! He just smiled and called them dumb cracks!

Bobby was from the hill district a troublesome community close to where I was from. I looked up to Bobby right away. After the cheering and bonuses were done it was time to go to work. When we all got down to the parking lot Todd showed me Bobby's car. It was a Jaguar; I had never seen a car quite like it. Even his plates reflected how rich he was as they said, 'YRUPOOR.' We all hung out for a while and played hacky-sack. I wasn't very good but it was still fun enough. After a time they called us all together and has us pile into four vans.

I was out with Chris on my first day of course my trainer Todd was there as well. We stopped at a 7-11 I don't remember what I got to eat but Todd gave me five bucks and five minutes to get something. He told me that if I didn't sell I would owe it back to him double. Well we left quickly after that and arrived a short time later at our territory in Manhattan Beach. I was really excited to be by the beach I had never even seen it before. Todd and I jumped out of the van and unloaded the four bottles of cleaner and two gallon refills and also several spray bottles to do demos with. We started going door to door and began pitching to people. I found that I was a natural and loved talking to people. I picked up quickly as I watched Todd sell and do demos each one lasting about two hours, drops, we called them. He then se me off on my own to see what I could do.

I took up the large bag of materials Todd gave me and started off. The bag was heavy and unless you were selling you got tired of carrying it around. I sold two quarts right off the bat and was happy quite proud of myself about it. I returned to the drop off area and met Chris who picked us up. I handed him my pick up slip and he smiled at me. "Good Job boy now get in." Was all he said to me however? As I got in the van everyone started high filing me when Chris said I popped my cheery, whatever that meant. I was so tired at that point I hardly cared it seemed as if it was a good thing. I was not used to carrying the cleaning materials on my shoulders. I about died when I heard that we still had three more hours of selling left to do yet which seemed ridicules. The next drop I sold absolutely nothing but at that point I could care less. They picked me back up and we went and picked up the other agents before heading back to the hotel.

We got back at around eight fifteen that evening. I went to Chris who was in charge of us at the time he gave me twenty bucks and said if I wanted more sell more. He still kind of laughed though as he said it as if he meant something more. There was a non-quota meeting at ten thirty. The meetings would take place often led by different people mainly the old heads. (Those were the people who had been there at least a year.) I ran into my brother after the meeting and found that he hadn't sold anything at all and as most brothers do I rubbed it in a little. After that Todd took me to the store to get beers and food.

Todd took me aside then and made me his friend as he called it and told me not to worry about the five bucks I got from him early that morning. When we got back with the food and booze everyone was in the wreck room and we started partying and having fun. It wasn't what I had expected it to be but I still though that this was the best job ever. I could not have been more wrong. My biggest dream was to become like Chris or Bobby and make lots of money and have lots of woman. What young man doesn't?

The next morning my brother and Rick quit I didn't even get a chance to talk to them about it. Chris told me that this job was not for them and quickly put me back to work. I thought they were nuts and stayed. The days became harder and easier the more you sold the more you got paid if you didn't sell you didn't get paid. Needless to say I had to sleep on the floor more than once. One day Bobby showed up with Ms. Crane who turned out to be his mistress along with a man named Steve who claimed to be a porn star. No one really seemed to confirm it or care though.

The days went by so fast I forgot about everything back home and didn't even call home. All I cared about was selling and partying. It had become my life and I had become lost within its seductive call. I quickly became brainwashed which was a sad truth that had happened to many kids my own age. Almost all of us were high school drop outs. I became good friends with a lot of the people as the days dragged on always the same as before. I felt as if they were my family and in many ways I felt closer to them than my real family. It was not all fun and games and like any family there was fighting and yelling and a few times I even took the blunt end of it. People came and went all of it like a steady flow. After a few months I started drinking a lot and I smoked a lot of pot it just became everyone's daily grind. But it was hard, we worked twelve hour days six day a week with little pay and on Sundays we did laundry.

Chapter Two

Brainwashed

**Bettor robbed, killed
after bragging of winnings**

9 LOS ANGELES — A man w
demanded cash after winn
$88,000 at the racetrack a
bragged of his luck was confron
in his flashy sportscar by a g
man who shot him to death a
stole his winnings, police s
Monday.

Romans 6:23; for the wages of sin is death but the gift of God is eternal life in Christ Jesus our Lord.

I couldn't leave even if I wanted to. I was good at Making sales and if you were good at it. They talked you into staying, no matter what they wouldn't let you go. I was in truth stuck. Months went by when we had a meeting at Bobby's house a meeting I later regretted gone to it. While I was there another agent came in and Bobby started beating him very bad. I was very scared and then I remembered my father's beatings all too well. Just hope I would never be the one receiving those. But of course I couldn't avoid them for long.

About a week after that meeting I was officially working on the Magazine Crew for six months. Our van pulled in after the long day of work we heard that some guys over heard a phone call to the car handler asking what had happened to Bobby. Chris told Todd to tell us to say nothing of course. He told us that if any of us brought it up would be fired with no bus fare to get, home essentially it shut us all up.

Chris called us all together shortly after that for an emergency meeting. He informed us that Bobby had been murdered at the race track after he won over $88,000. He won the Superfecta and the Quadfecta all in the same day at Hollywood Park Casino in Los Angeles. What are the chances of that happening? He demanded cash for his all of his winnings. They wanted to write him a check but he didn't listen. He was very intimidating and a very large man and did not take no for an answer. So they gave him the cash.

Steve the president of the Magazine Crew I was on. He told me years later that someone had watched him collect the money and decided to follow him and he was killed by a single shot threw his heart in broad daylight! A single 22 caliper bullet. Right in front of the lobby entrance at Stoffer's Hotel close to LAX airport. I once went by there with Steve about 10 years later. The bell-hop that witnessed it, still remembered the event like it was yesterday. It was so unreal to go there and have someone talk about it.

I had mixed emotions about his death. Bobby had always been nice to me but he was still a ruthless man and had a bad gambling problem. We suspected that one of the local casinos was responsible for it but we never did find out for sure he did owe them a lot of money. The sad part of it was that the guy who did it only served seven years in prison for it. The whole crew went to Bob's funeral. It was a big event a lot of people where there. Bob's brother took over the crew shortly thereafter and almost everyone save me and eighteen other guys left.

Recently I spoke to Ron a manager for Bobby at the time of his death. He told me he was in the passenger seat of the car with Bob when he got shot. He said the gunman unloaded the whole clip in the car. The bullets just barely missed his head and he was lucky to be alive. There was the cash flying everywhere. The gun man walked around to the passenger side of the jaguar. Ron felt a cold presence that instantly came across his shoulder. He thanks god that he survived and for some reason none of the bullets hit him. He's father is a bishop of church. His prayers I think that had something to do with him not getting shot. He also remembered a guy named "JIMMY THE MOUTH" that's the horse timer they had flown in from Philadelphia the day before the race. Apparently he was well connected to the mob. His cut was 10% of the action. Ron and another acquaintance named Mannie split the purse three ways. Unfortunately Bob was the one that really lost. Leaving behind two children and an ex-wife to raise the kids by herself. Another person I traveled with said the bigger win was supposed to come the next day. I do not know much truth there is to that last statement.

Ron also told me that in the 70's and 80's the mob laundered there money threw the crews because in was all cash business. How it worked was the mob bosses would pay the magazine managers 10%. They would give thim cash for cash. The agent's draws and hotels would get paid with mob money because they traveled city to city. I wonder how much of that ended up paying for drugs and strippers. It was next to impossible for them to get caught. Finding this out they were probably still in bed together in the 90's. Just thinking with Bobby having a friend named "JIMMY THE MOUTH".

The cleaning division of the crew dies along with Bobby. Chris took over it and made it a Magazine division. One of the people who stayed was a guy named Bud he took over my training and started teaching me how to sell magazines.

We did not know it but Chris had plans of his own and none of us knew anything about Bobby's brother and none of us really wanted to work for him. Chris took the opportunity and gathered a group meeting and announced that he was going to start his own crew. He said that if w joined with him we would move West Hollywood and sell out of Cadillac's. All of us were sick of selling for the new boss and we all jumped on the opportunity.

Chris started a new crew and shortly after we all left Bobby's old crew went out of business entirely. Chris took us to the Ramada Hotel in West Hollywood on Sunset Blvd. It was a massive culture shock. There were gay people everywhere not that I'm homophobic but it was a little unnerving. Bud got right on with training us on how to sell magazines and we were off once again. It was a lot harder to do cause instead of knocking on peoples doors we now walked up to people in the streets.

It was also a lot harder to get business at first cause unlike before where we showed off the product and the customer got it them and there now they had to wait and only had our word on the subscriptions that they would even get the magazines. We were taught to sell no matter what even if it meant us making up random stories like 'I'm trying to earn money to go to college' or 'trying to start our own businesses or even 'Trying to win a trip to Europe.' Everyone had their own pitch and one guy even said he was a Christian student trying to raise money. My warning to you is be very careful before buying from anyone they could tell you anything and will just to make that sale.

My pitch was that I had to collect a twenty thousand point record in ten weeks and if I did I would win five thousand dollars to spend anyway I would like. Of course they were all a bunch of lies and not a single thing was true. We only barley got paid in commissions. But still I began to look up to Bud especially when he took me to sell one day at Ventura Blvd. in Woodland Hills and sold to twenty people in less than three hours which was very impressive. Moreover the woman loved him and he was dating the hottest girl in the crew a fine lady named Michelle. Bud's biggest advantage however was that he was a great Canvasser (A great speaker in Magazine Crew talk.) I envied the man I could hardly make two to five sales a day and I couldn't hook up with a girl to save my life even one of the crew's girls. But Bud did teach me how to be confident while making sales which helped me a lot.

Bud later became an executive producer in Hollywood and now owns his own company. He does credit some of his success for the things he learned from Bobby. But he recently told me Bobby owed him $20,000 that he sued Bob's estate and they never paid him. Bud also went through a lot of abuse on the crew. I heard Bobby beat him up pretty one time.

The days started blending in again and we all started partying a lot more now that Bobby wasn't around anymore to keep everyone in line. Bobby never did believe in drinking or doing drugs. A few days of this went by and I eventually borrowed some of Bud's clothes because I had nothing nice to wear and it would help me make sales. Selling cleaner never made me much money so I couldn't buy any new clothes. He let me borrow them and dropped me off in Twin oaks and made a few more sales than normal and I was also able to get myself a date. *I guess having nice clothes does pay off,* I remember thinking to myself.

She didn't live to far away from our hotel and I had her come and pick me up. I had to meet her across the street because it was against the crew rules to let anyone outside the crew to know where we were staying. This rule was specifically enforced when dealing with cops; who always kicked us out of malls and other places for soliciting. None of us got the hint of it though. Anyway she took me back to her condo and made me take off all of my clothes. I doubt I need to say anything more. The whole experience gave me mixed emotions considering the girl took pictures of me after we had been together and then just as quickly dropped me off at like two in the morning at the hotel.

I was way late for our curfew and Chris was ticked and fined me my bonus money I had coming to me the next morning. I hardly cared I was at that moment just happy I finally got laid. Regardless of everything that had happened I now had no doubt that this job was perfect for me. I thought it was great not even hear a year and already I got laid and was able to party and have fun. My God I was so I! Anyway I was also so drunk at the time that I didn't sell anything the next day I was a WAB (WAB means Weak Ass Bitch) pardon my French. Well the others in the crew didn't like it and showed their respects for me at a gas station we stopped at later that day.

They picked me up and doused me with the window cleaning fluid and used me to clean the windows. I was so ticked. They even rubbed it all over my mouth and face. All Chris said was that I deserved it for Wabbing all day. He then said it was either that or loses my job and he wouldn't pay my way home. I wasn't about to lose my job so I left the matter as it was. Bud was not happy about it and a few days later quit and took his girlfriend with him. So I was stuck selling with my old mentor Todd.

Things were fine at first until I started out selling him and Chris started mocking him about it. I was beginning to become an excellent salesman and I knew it. Todd left the crew himself a little while later but stole about five agents when he left. Chris was so pissed. Todd took them to

Florida to work for another company. Such was the Magazine Crew business everyone plotted against each other's backs at least those who had some power that is. And both Chris and Todd wanted to be like Bobby and have the power and all that jazz.

Todd left Chris with me a guy named Chaz three new guys. Our entire group of female salesman followed Todd. It was no matter however I started selling a lot and made up for most of the profit loss. I felt good. I was making a lot more money now and was able to buy my own clothes and my sales pitches were like hotcakes, almost everyone bought them. I began telling everyone anything to make a sale.

Eventually Ms. Crane showed up and started dating Chris again I often wondered if he was doing some heavy drugs because he started to sniff a lot. I could hardly doubt it a lot of the guys were doing it a lot since Bobby died I figured why not Chris. My suspicions were proven correct when Chris started acting like a jerk if you didn't sell enough. And he began paying us next to nothing again. He also stopped holding our daily meetings and confined himself to his room. We suffered three weeks of it before Todd showed back up with his own crew. He wanted me to work for him and promised me things would be better with him than before. In the end the girls with him talked me into to it I was sucker for woman. So one day after we made our arrangement and Chris was drugged out with Ms. Crane Todd pulled up behind the hotel so Chris wouldn't see us leave and loaded up the rest of the crew. Todd took us to where he was staying and we met back up with bud. We all partied all night to celebrate.

The next morning Todd took us to the airport to leave for Florida and Chris showed up with the cops and said we stole from him. Unknown to me one of the girls took Chris' pager and stuffed it into my bag the cops took it and placed me in a cell down town. I lost it I had never been in a prison before in my life and I was still drunk from the night before. I started throwing up all over my cell and pounding on the walls I was so scared I didn't know what to do with myself. But after four hours the girls talked to the cops and they let me go. They convinced the cops that Chris was lying and they started questioning him. Needless to say it gave us enough time to leave and get on the plane to Florida.

When we got to Florida Todd took us to our hotel and I was happy to see Todd, Todd was happy to have someone he knew would make me some money. I had never been to Florida and I was happy to be away from Chris he had become a drug addict. Everything seemed fine a first but I started to see a Magazine Crew pattern emerge. Todd started drinking a lot already not a good sign. He built up our crew to about forty people. Todd made me his crew leader and I was in charge of training everyone. I spent two years running the crew and trying to keep it together while Todd got more and more messed up. After two years however the crew fell apart.

A lot of people began to leave mainly because Todd started waving around his gun a lot when he got drunk. Word started getting out and we started getting a lot of cancellations on our orders. Of course Todd blamed me and one day called me in his room and beat the living tar out of me. He had never done that to me before. I knew he was capable of it he used to have a black guy named Dana that he used to call into the room just to beat him but never me. I felt betrayed.

I felt bad for Dana of course but I figured it was better him than me. So Todd began to take a new selling approach and beat anyone who didn't sell. Greed consumed him and he became a monster. But I stayed mainly out of fear of leaving. Todd worked out his differences with Chris who joined back up under Todd and things started getting a little better but we traveled a lot more now from state to state, town to town. It was a hard life and I was beginning to forget myself.

I was still among the top dogs and Todd let me party with him and Chris. I started doing coke and meth with them and we were drinking hard every night. I didn't even know myself anymore at that point. My new rue teen consisted of working all day and getting paid in drugs at night I became one of their slaves. Eventually we ended back up in California and we were staying in Northridge when the earthquakes started. It flipped me out so Chris and Todd proposed we head for Hawaii for a short break on things. I agreed of course still feeling empty still wanting to get away from it all. I still felt helpless and I desperately wanted peace. So I agreed and fifteen of us all took off for Hawaii.

We spent three weeks there and it turned out to be a goldmine and sold almost thirty three sales per day. To reward me Todd bought me a solid gold ring. He also hired us a guy named Drake to drive us around it was real sweet. I remember one night Drake, Todd, Chris, and I were all smoking crack and one of us left a hot pipe in one of our rooms at the hotel and it nearly burned the whole place down. Todd was ticked and blamed us though he was smoking too. Todd still blamed me and picked me up in his car and began beating me up again. He beat me so bad I wanted to quit. My head was bleeding so bad and my shirt full of blood from my lips. It took my eyes like a month to heal.

I wasn't sure how to having been there in the crew for almost four years now and I had never once in all of that time called my family. I hated the thought that my father might think I had failed and that hurt more than the beating. I swallowed my pride and stayed however after Todd apologized to me and took me to a strip club to make things up to me. It was still hard after that and even worse trying to sell with a black eye. We would have stayed longer but the cops kicked us off the island and forced s to go back to California.

To second back in California the Halloween season came along. The night before we were all parting pretty hard. We were all out by the swimming pool of the hotel dinking. All of sudden Jason a guy on the crew got struck with a crowbar in his by a rival crew. He was bleeding so bad and had a large hole on the side of his neck. It was crazy I ran to Todd's room and quickly told him. There was about 4 guys in a pick up truck with bats and weapons.

They jumped out and started swinging and hit another guy. Chris and Todd ran out with guns but the rival crew quickly fled. Jason was once stabbed in Vegas a year before. It took him 2 weeks to heal. Jason loved to fight and was not afraid of anybody he protected me many times. Were ever Jason is today I would like to thank him for protecting me.

I remember working a parking lot with a girl named Angie. I spoke to her a couple months back and she recalled this event. A woman had left the parking lot of a grocery store. She had left her purse in the shopping cart I was having a bad day in sales. So I took the purse hoping there was cash left in it and there was. I went to take it and suddenly the lady returned so I quickly returned the purse to her she was so happy. The cops were in the parking lot and came up to me and Angie. They asked us what we were doing there. We said selling magazines they were upset and was going to take us both to jail for stealing the ladies purse. Apparently someone seen me take it and put in the crew van. I took blame it was all mine anyway. I am glad they let Angie go. I did 2 weeks in jail for that mistake when I got out Todd was really upset. That is the first time I ever did something like that. I just didn't want to face Todd without my quota. Sorry Angie!

We started traveling again almost as soon as we got back and the days began to drag on and on. O really didn't want to do it anymore. But I was trapped. We eventually made it back to Florida by the time I finally told Todd I was done spinning my wheels working for him and needed a break. It had almost been five years now. I went into his room he was smoking a joint so I smoked it with him he told me not to worry that he would pay for my trip home. He told me to relax at the hotel and when the rest of the agents got back he would send someone to take me to the bus. The calm manner in which he said it scared me and I went straight to a cop who helped me get away from them and protect me. I was in such a hurry that I forgot my things.

I went back to get them but Todd met me with his gun in hand. He said he wanted the watch and ring he had given me back at Hawaii. I could care less and asked for a ticket home. He said that it was waiting for me back at the bus station. I grabbed my things and took off not wanting to stay any longer. The cop I had befriended took me to the station and made sure I got on the bus. It turned out that my father who I hadn't so much as talked to in five years had paid for my ticked after Todd had called him. God bless that cop he saved me from Todd.

I never did see Todd again I heard some rumors that he was thrown in jail for fraud and slavery. I only regretted not being able to testify against him that man had put me through hell. I ended back up in Pittsburgh my father wanted little to do with me so my grandparents took me in. They got me a job at Bally's Health Club which didn't last long. Staying with my grandparents didn't last long either. So my dad helped me get a small apartment in Southside near 23rd street right next to a bar.

I was so depressed and still felt void inside and out. I began drinking my problems away. After about a month Chris got a hold of me and like a dummy I went back. He flew me out to California again. He wasn't traveling with Todd anymore I started selling with him again for almost a year. We never stopped partying and that year he took me up to Lake Tahoe for Christmas and New Years. It was the one good perk to the business you got to go to a lot of really cool places. Ricky was on Chris's crew when I got there me and me Ricky once sold together. So I kind of knew him but we were on different crews at one point.

Ricky was from Duncan Oklahoma, we hit it off right away. Ricky and I liked to party hard and chase after girls we sold too. I am not sure if I envied him or wanted to be like him. He pretty much got any girl he wanted. We ended up leaving Chris and going to work for Steve Bob's old friend. When we got there he had a ski boat and took us out knee boarding I thought Steve was pretty cool. He said he was going to make us both managers but I didn't believe him. There were too girls on the crew at the time Jennifer and Genoa. Jennifer liked Ricky automatically and liked Genoa. Genoa was sleeping with Steve when he was married the Mia at the time. He loved young girls and from what I heard recently he has not changed. He would lure the new girls to watch porn and drink in his room. Genoa I know for a fact was hooked on coke. Pretty easy preye for the boss "Steve".

One day we got back to the hotel after a bad day in sales. Ricky went in to Steve's room with the car sheet (that's the sales totals for the crew) Steve flipped out because we had a bad day. Imagine that! He started throwing stuff around he's room and yelling at all of us.

I was use to this type of behavior it comes with the job of the Magazine business. Later that night, Ricky came into my room and said the girls and him were leaving. They wanted me to come so we could start our own crew. I desperately wanted that, so I went along with it. We had to leave with out Steve catching us. I remember what Todd put me through.

So Jennifer's parents picked us up down the street at like 3:00 am we were all pretty scared of Steve. Well we got to there home and they were very welcoming. I loved her family they were nothing like mine. The next her dad gave us some money to start our new crew and a car. Me and Ricky printed up some receipts and sales materials. We kept some materials from Steve's crew to copy. Genoa told me the FBI stopped her in a parking lot and questioned her about Steve the day after we printed up our new materials. Craziness! I am glad we split before Steve went down.

We began selling in Fort Worth and Dallas making a lot of cash quick. I starting pressing Ricky to get a clearance deal for a company so we can send the magazines off to the customers. I wanted people to get what they paid for because I know for a fact Todd never sent his customers there magazines. Ricky was a control freak and told me the company was only going to be in his name. We fought about it for about a week but I didn't care. Genoa was starting to like me and that's really what cared about. I was always looking for love.

Ricky decided we should go to Oklahoma City to sell because his parents lived close to there. I wanted to build the crew up so I hired a couple of kids off the street pretty easy. Now there was 6 of us selling Ricky started acting like Steve it was kind of funny at first but in the end he screwed up our friendship. The two new guys didn't sell anything on there 3rd day so Ricky wanted to be the big boss and fire them. What a dumb move without agents you are not a boss.

We packed it up and went back to Fort Worth and stayed with Jennifer' parents once again. Ricky saved up like $1,000 when we got there he talked Jennifer' parents into buying a Ford Bronco it was white. Ricky's credit was bad because he wrote a lot of bad checks. I will explain later! I was so lost at this point we stayed hi and were messing with meth again. We got the truck Ricky gave her parents the cash he had as a down payment. He was a master manipulator the best I ever known.

Ricky now wanted to hit the road state to state. Jennifer and he started fighting a lot. Genoa and I did most of the sales and Genoa didn't want to sell anymore. I didn't mind it that's all I have ever done it was like my college education. Pretty said I know. Ricky fired Genoa once again he thought he was the boss. I was upset she left but she really did not like me I was just someone that was there to her.

Ricky wanted to stop in Duncan were he was from to get a DBA for the company so he could cash checks. At the bank he told me I should open an account to save money. I agreed and did it! Really Ricky had other intentions. When Ricky was 16 him and his brother stole a bunch of checks and flew to Hawaii and forged $20,000 worth on everything imaginable. He told me that story when I first met him but I never believed him. He was finally telling me the truth about something. He said if you don't want to sell I know another way to make more money. So of course I went along with it. We ended up in Vegas we went out and went of a check writing spree. Chalking up $30,000 in cash , clothes , stereo for the truck you name it we had it. We wanting everything are old bosses had. Big mistake! Big mistake!

About 2 months go by we partied the money away on

gambling and drugs. They put out warrants in the city where we opened the accounts. I was totally convinced Ricky was a Con-Man I knew I had to get away for him. I told him I was going out to sell and never returned I left all the stuff behind I didn't care about it. We stole it all of it. I called up Chris and told him what happened and bought me a bus ticket to California. Here we go again! At the bus station Ricky showed up with the police and said I stole his sales book. Well the cop seen through Ricky and let me on the bus lucky for me he didn't run my name. Finally free of Ricky!

Several years later I was running a ad for Steve and ran into Jennifer she said Ricky went to Jail and lost the truck. I knew it. He had her brainwashed for far too long. Ricky had also called my parents after I left and said I died and they had to wire him $1,000 to send the body home. What a loser. He knew I didn't keep in contact with them. I didn't find this out till three months later. Jennifer is now married and has two kids she looked great when I saw her.

I was good to be back around Chris he wasn't as violent as Steve and as crazy as Ricky. I started selling right away. Chris was happy to have me back we build a pretty solid crew. I still was hooked on meth but didn't do any for a couple of days. I was selling at USC College one day after a night of pretty heavy drinking and smoking meth. I felt like my heart was about to stop it was beating so hard. I was really scared like I thought I was going to die. I went to the hospital and when I got there I was stressed. They finally took me I thought I was going to die in the waiting room. They quick ask me what I was on and I told them. So they gave me something to reverse the drugs I was on. Thank God! When I woke up the doctor said I was lucky that my heart could have stopped. That was the last time I ever touched that drug.

I was dating a girl named Ana at that time and while we were out partying one day I ran into Steve again I was scared at first but he really did not care that I with left with Ricky.

He told me that he was starting his own crew again and would like for me to join. He whipped out a wad of one hundred dollar bills and told me it could all be mine. I wasn't sure about it cause Steve's wife had recently left him and took with her almost twenty thousand dollars. She had been a stripper and left the first chance she got. He was real bitter about it and I wasn't sure about getting involved. He said if I changed my mind to give him a call. Chris took us to LA to sell and after two weeks I still felt empty so I gave him a call. He was excited and told me I was to be his manager.

That caught my attention I always wanted to be a manager. I left in the middle of the day my last day with Todd was still fresh in my mind despite it being almost a whole year come and gone. I didn't want to face Chris back at the hotel so I just left. I left losing everything. It wasn't the first time nor would it be my last to lose everything. I got back on the Greyhound bus and headed for San Diego. Steve had wired me a ticket I left Ana behind I knew she was cheating on me so I didn't really care. Once there I went back to Lake Tahoe.

When I got there Steve let me stay on an air mattress in his living room. He let me borrow a lot of cloths seeing as I had left all of my own back in California. Two days later I was back out in the streets selling magazines for yet another magazine scam. Steve was able to recruit six girls and a guy named Darrel and his girlfriend Julie. Steve bought of a piece of crap van for like a thousand bucks which Darrel crashed the second day. I trained everyone and became close to one of the girls their named Tailor. We did all of the work while Steve stayed at home and reaped the benefits of our labor while he claimed to sell the magazines we knew he was a liar. It caused unrest in our new crew. Steve might have once been Bobby's right hand man but he knew nothing of selling things. Still he sold everything he had in storage and sold some time shares until we had enough money to hit the road. That was when we went to Oakland and stayed. I still wonder why I went back to work for Steve.

Chapter Three

Lost, Trapped and Stuck

Galatians 5:19-21; For the works of the flesh are evident which are: adultery, fornication, uncleanness, lawlessness, idolatry, sorcery, hatred, contentions, jealousy, outburst of wrath, selfish ambitions, dissension, heresy, envy, murders, drunkenness, revelries, and the like will by no means enter heaven

The Jack London Inn in Oakland was the ghetto of all ghetto hotels. The place was crawling with danger, with gangs and hot tempered drug dealers. There were also pimps and their prostitutes. And for over a week all of them were my neighbors. I finally got to drive our car, everyone called me the car handler. I was now in charge of drop offs and pick ups. I did really well with my new job and Steve paid me more money than I ever even saw before. I liked Steve a lot better than Todd or Chris he didn't do drugs and Steve would take me to a lot of strip bars. What could I say I was young?

Steve did help me pay off the warrants I collected with Ricky. I ended up doing 3 weeks in jail when I first got back to crew. Of course I had to pay him back but in the magazine business when the manager does something nice for you there is a price to pay. Steve never did something kind because he wanted to it was because he had to it was to benefit him. The positive thing is they withdraw it all from my record. He also helped me pay a bunch of tickets so I could get my drivers license back. Once again he needed someone to drive the agents around. I also paid him back for that. In the magazine industry there is always a price to pay even when you get out of it.

Right off the bat Steve hired a beautiful girl named

Tiffany and I instantly fell in love with her, or at least I thought I did. I hooked up with her almost right away too and she would go and party with me and the crew. Steve wasn't very happy about that cause he didn't like us being with any of the new girls. He said that if you dated a new girl it would mess up their minds and they won't sell as well as before. But I didn't care and neither did she. Tiffany had a good friend named Jimmy who joined our crew shortly after we started dating.

The crew got big fast. Steve always used to reward us by taking us out to the movies or play softball on the weekends which was always fun. But still during the week it was always the same. Sell, sell, sell twelve hours a day from eight in the morning to eight at night. Besides the weekends everything stayed the same people came and went and I was still one of the top dogs. Mine and Tiffany's relationship grew and we both thought we were in love, maybe we were. Steve and Darrel were planning on taking a trip to Hawaii and I was still kind of wary about it cause of last time. Jimmy convinced me to go though I was his trainer and we had become very good friends he told me it would be different that this time we would be going to Maui.

Things were great in Maui that was until Steve and Darrel told me I had won a bonus fishing trip to one of the other islands. They said that I could go and get away for a few days with no work and just relax. Well that was partially true but three days after I left I came back to find that they had all left without me and without a ticket home. Well I stayed on the beach for like three days after I ran out of money for a hotel. I was there by myself for a week until Steve called me up. He told me it was all Darrel's idea. Steve told me that he got rid of Darrel and that he would pay me for my ticket back home. When I got back to the crew Steve said he was sorry and explained why he had done it.

According to Steve he had done it to earn Darrel's trust so he could get rid of him. I guess Steve had made Darrel his partner and was tired of splitting all of the profits with him. Things kind of went back to normal after that I accepted Steve's apology and went to go see Tiffany I missed her terribly and so did she. Then my recurring nightmare started all over again sell, sell, sell. That was my life. I was so tired of it by that time I started to save all of my money. I was making a lot back then since Steve had me on a higher commission. I spent the next six months doing this. At the end of that time Jimmy and his girl friend Taylor they moved back up to Tahoe. The night after they left Tiffany was missing when I went to go look for her I found her and a guy named Tommy having sex. I flipped out I ran back to the hotel and punched in a window.

The strange thing of it was I still loved her and forgave her. I told her we should leave the crew and go live with Jimmy and Taylor we needed to be away from all of this crap. She agreed and we planned our escape. We left at like three in the morning we were terrified that Steve might find out but he never did. We arrived in Tahoe on another Greyhound bus and we moved in with Jimmy. He had gotten a job selling time shares for a Tahoe ski and beach resort and he was able to get me a job there too. We did pretty well and made decent money. But that's when I began to develop yet another addiction. Gambling! There were several casinos nearby which we blew all of our money as soon as we got it.

A month went by and Steve finally got a hold of us again. He said that he had fired Tommy and he wanted us to hire people for him in Tahoe. He also said all was forgiven and if we wanted to come back we could come back. We agreed to hire people for him but Jimmy and I were partying a lot at that time and we didn't want to go back. Tiffany left then for a week t visit her family I missed her something terrible. When she got back however she was not pleased to find out that both Jimmy and I got fired from our last job cause we didn't show up to work for a couple of days. We did get hired on selling cars however which cooled her temper a bit.

Selling cars though only lasted about two weeks. I didn't care because I had found out something that scared and excited me to death. Tiffany was pregnant. I got myself another job and we got our own place I could hardly believe I was going to be a dad. I was a salesman again and I would have to leave town a lot to promote my product and Tiffany was still hiring people for Steve together we were making it. But Tiffany wanted to go back home to Indiana to be with her mom I fought with her about it. Jimmy had started a new Crew and I wanted to stay and help him run it. Jimmy and I fought about it so I decided to leave.

I called up Steve his crew was in New York and I told him I would come back and he paid for my ticket there. On the way there I noticed that my bus stopped near Chi-town near where Tiffany was staying. I called her up and she asked me to come and live with her I did of course. I stayed there for about two weeks. I loved her family they were all really nice to me. But Tiffany was becoming distant. She would often times go out at night until two or three in the morning. She was also drinking a lot despite the fact that she was pregnant it broke my heart. She made it worse by telling me it wasn't my kid anyway. It broke me.

I called up Steve again and I wanted to get away from all the pain. Steve was pissed off at me for not showing up like I said I was. So I went back home to Pittsburgh and stayed with my dad. Steve moved his crew there however and I started selling for him again. I was so tired of woman and people I let myself get lost in my job. Steve eventually brought back Darrel which I hated for leaving me in Hawaii. We worked out our differences however and Steve promoted me to manager again. I was able to save up enough money to buy my own car which brought me a little happiness. I became sick and lonely and started getting really drunk and I started messing around with the crew girls. Steve was tired of my behavior and demoted me so I split again and went back home for the third time.

I moved back into my brother's house it had been the first time I had seen them since they left the first crew. They told me that Bobby had lied to me ad had not bought them tickets home. Instead he gave them ten bucks and left them there. They were stranded for over a week. I was so mad I couldn't see straight I what had I gotten myself into? I got another job this time as a telemarketer which didn't really work out. My brother got married though and moved in with his new bride. I was happy and a little jealous of him. It brought back memories I would have rather forgotten. Anyway it just left me and Rick.

Don't ask me how or why but Steve somehow got my number again and called me. I was brainwashed and going crazy at the time. He said that if I came back and stayed a solid year he would give me a Rolex and a new car. He also said that there was a hot girl there named Leia which I would like. Needless to say I went back, and found that Steve was right Leia was hot!! The crew was now in Nashville and I started dating Leia right away and which made Steve pretty angry at me cause of his no dating new girls rule thing. But Steve told me that as long as she met her quota she could stay in my room.

There was only about five guys in the crew at this time Steve had not been running his business very well which was one of the reasons he wanted me back. It was fine for a while Steve found himself a girl and he seemed happier. I ask Jimmy if he would join me I needed help getting the crew bigger he said yes. As the crew was getting bigger so did Steve's appetite for money. He started getting ticked if you didn't make your quota and would ban you from the girl you liked it sucked. He always blamed me I there was something that didn't go quite right. He even wanted me to hold an hour long meeting after a twelve hour day I did it of course but it wasn't fun.

One night Steve and Jimmy were out partying real bad. I had just got to my room wanted to relax for a while when he called me to his room. He was pissed and he beat me up and chipped my tooth and through me in a shower, said I deserved it because of something Jimmy did. The next morning Steve apologized and gave me that Rolex he promised me. I still hated the fact that he beat me Todd used to do that and that was why I left him. But Steve knew how to get back n my good side and knew how to work me so I stayed.

The crew started growing bigger and I was a lot of

money nowhere near as much Steve was but I was really happy just being with Leia. I knew that Leia wasn't being faithful to me; sleeping around with customers and others on the crew. But I was so messed up at that point I didn't care. I just went to more and more strip clubs. We were all living the same lies to us it was all about the money. That is the way the Magazine business is. Steve started treating Leia like crap because she was always doing drugs and running off. I didn't care anymore she was cheating on me left and right.

I still took her to Hawaii though for a week. We even went to a party and Hulk Hogan was there with us he turned out to be a real dick. Still the trip was really good and I think I will always remember it. After we got back to the crew it was right back to the grind. Leia ended up leaving the crew in Vegas and went on to become a porn star. Her porn name is Cameron Caine and she is very famous now. It was a sad ending to a really nice person. But I hooked up with another girl on the crew that I had been messing around with her name was Coriee. We ended up staying together for almost seven years on and off the road and even started our own crew.

We started with twenty four agents and I made nearly three thousand dollars a day. This shocked me considering Todd told me I would never amount to anything and I doubted myself that I could ever make it running my own crew. I was wrong and so was Todd I ended up breaking every record he had ever set. After all of that success Coriee and I ended up in Florida for Christmas we had been out of Steve's crew at the time for nearly six months. We thought we were going to do fine until Jimmy showed up at our doorstep and started beating me I thought he was going to kill me. We took off to Pensacola were we stayed with a Christian friend of mine he helped us out a lot.

Steve was mad at Jimmy and sent our stuff to us that we left at the hotel the night Jimmy beat on me. Some of Coriee's things were missing though and she blamed me. But I wasn't about to go and face Jimmy or Steve they were crazy. Things started to really change for almost eight months I was going to church and Coriee and I were real close. One day Darrel called me and said that Steve had stranded him and needed help. I wanted to help him so I bought him a ticket. I always knew Darrel was a shady guy but I decided to trust him when he said we should sell everything and head to the Virgin Isles. So I sold my house and all my valuables and jumped on a plane and went.

I had already had a job all lined up selling time shares when I got there. We rented a small apartment which wasn't big enough for the three of us so Darrel went his own way. Coriee and I ended up getting a nice car and a condo right off the beach in Megan Bay in St. Thomas. Darrel moved in with us and within a week we were almost completely broke. When we did have extra money we partied it away. Darrel ended up getting a job but I was having trouble selling time shares. I eventually got fired and got a job cleaning boats at eight dollars an hour.

Eight dollars an hour was the poorest of poor in this island paradise and we eventually had to move out of the condo which was like two thousand dollars a month. Darrel found us another place which had a good view of the

Islands. We ended up buying a lot of weed from a nearby gas station and we got high all the time. It was kind of funny we were the only white guys on the island but we were well loved by everyone. Coriee eventually got a job at a beach resort and between the three of us we were making it really well.

Coriee worked the front desk and one day met a girl named Paula who wanted a quick date. Coriee told her of our roommate Darrel and they hit it off right away. Two days later Darrel shows up with like ten thousand dollars in cash and said that Paula was going to buy him a boat so they could open up a charted business. And the extra cash was for anything we needed.

So I quit my job I hated it anyway and Darrel and Paula went down and picked out a boat which Paula paid for in cash. I was to be Darrel's first mate. I could hardly believe what was going on we barely knew the lady. Paula had to go home after that but Darrel promised her that he would get the whole thing started for her. We started canvassing the beached looking for people to take around the islands. I was good at it and we charged five hundred dollars a day we did it about once a week. The rest of the time Darrel and I would go fishing.

We caught a lot of fish and had a blast. One day Darrel asked me if I would fly to St. Croix and go Gambling and golfing with him. I asked him how we were going to do that we barely had enough to get by. He smiled and said that we would use the bank roll Paula had given him. She had said it was for things we needed. He said that who cared what we did with it she was gone all we had to do was park the boat and get on the plane. I was stupid enough to listen to him. We got down there and Darrel got us the most expensive suit in the nicest hotel at like three hundred and fifty dollars a night. It cost us almost two hundred dollars per round of golf and we spent over fifteen hundred gambling.

We burnt through the money so fast I wasn't sure

where it was going. I told Darrel he was crazy we should get back before Paula comes back and sees what we are doing. He said don't worry she isn't coming back for another month. Darrel told me that we could make it all back doing a bunch of charters. Well things didn't get any better the boat broke down and Darrel kelp spending money. He even bought a brand new dodge for forty thousand cash. He then fixed the boat and spent two hundred on supplies.

About a month later Paula returned Darrel was ready for her however and told her that everything was in order. He showed her the new truck and the equipment and even had a charter lined up for her so everything looked good. He even gave her the five hundred from the trip and told her that the rest had gone to repairs on the boat. The crazy thing of it was she believed him. I think it had to do with the fact that he got he so drunk she couldn't see straight. She left none the wiser. We started back to the same old stuff living off her while she thought everything was going good. I felt so bad I wanted to tell her everything but I was more afraid of Darrel he was a big guy and I didn't want him angry at me.

We did some charters just enough to fool Paula. Eventually she caught whiff of our dealings from a dock worker. Needless to say she was pissed and took our boat and the extra cash. Matters were made worse when Steve called Darrel and said he wanted to rent a boat for a day. Darrel agreed of course. It turned out that Steve had fired Jimmy who was on his way to prison and Steve wanted me and Coriee back. He didn't want Darrel so he never talked about it until we were alone. Coriee wanted to leave anyway so like a dummy I agreed to go back to prison in a since.

Steve told me after a surprisingly great weekend that he wanted me to call him about the job so Darrel wouldn't think we were going to leave him on the island. I got a temporary job working on boats while Steve would call me every day to help me plan how to best leave Darrel behind. But I eventually told him everything and he was pissed off but he eventually got over it and took it better than I thought he would. I kind of felt bad so I gave Darrel my last paycheck to help him find someplace to go and Coriee and I left for California once again.

So we get to our new home another hotel and we were thrust back into the whole relentless cycle of cash and sales. It started out real slow and we ran out of money real quick. I remember that I would stay and print off supplies and Coriee would sell and make us some money it was tuff. A lot of the crew didn't want us back which made things worse they were afraid of the competition and thought we would step of their toes which of course we were only too happy to oblige.

Steve also had a new guy running the crew a guy named Tony. He was an ok guy but like everyone in the crew he would stab you in the back first chance he got especially if it meant bettering his current predicament. Within less than six months I was outselling everyone and I was once again the unofficial top dog. Tony took over once he caught Steve sleeping around with Coriee I caught them myself. Just another heart break that hurt so bad, seven years obviously meant nothing to her.

I was going to leave Coriee but Tony convinced me that it wasn't worth it. He said it would be better for business if I stay with her and him through all of the strip clubs in my face and said it was no different. I now that he was right but at that point I hated him for it because he went to them too. So I swallowed my pain and went back to it business took off. The bad thing of it was that Tony would call me like ten times a day and yell at me if we had low sales. I did whatever I could; having the position thrust on me like that I even drove the agents around myself and tried to bolster sales but it was all in vain. I was glad when Tony quit after he got robbed at the hotel by a bunch of hookers. They stole his truck and a bunch of his money. I didn't feel sorry for him one bit.

I then took over all of the agents I was now in charge since Tony left. I made thirteen hundred dollars a day again and I loved it. Well I ran things pretty good for about six months and things were going really smooth. Of course my boss (no one really knew his real name we all called him Boss.) kept a close eye on things and made sure I made a deposit to him at exactly noon every day. He put a lot of stress on me and would harass me all the time. He took everything out on me even if he was fighting with his wife it was my fault! I just rolled with the punches I needed the work and I needed the money so I could get away for a while with Coriee.

Boss wanted us to bump up the sales and he said if I did he would give me the time off. We began planning a seven day trip we would spend three days in Pittsburgh with my family and four in Bakersfield with Coriee's. We bumped up his sales and he bought us the tickets. We left on our trip but right in the middle of it Boss called me and said he fired everyone and he has our stuff in Seattle. We were afraid to go back and the rest of our trip sucked.

Coriee's grandmother passed away while we were there and everything became a big mess.

Everyone knew that Coriee and I were out of a job and had nowhere to go. Fortunately I had my dad save some of my money for me. I had to drive back to Pittsburgh to get all of our things I was really pissed. I couldn't stop thinking about the crew I hated the Boss for sending us on vacation only to fire me. I felt really bad for the kids that got fired I had put a lot of time into them and most of them depended on it. A lot of the agents started calling me and Coriee asking what was going on they were all confused. Coriee told them to go home and we told them we would figure everything out. Well I ended up asking one of my old agents Jake if he would go with me to Pittsburgh with me to pick up my things he said yes.

Jake and I drove all the way to Pittsburgh from Seattle. My dad hooked us up with a house. Coriee was still grieving over her grandmother's death and was with her family back in Bakersfield. My plan was to get to

Pittsburgh and regroup the crew. So I called some of my old friends from the crew and I started my own business and I was surprised when my dad helped me get started. Within a week I had eight people and my crew started a very successful magazine business. It was harder than I thought it would be and I was still uncertain about myself since Steve messed me over.

I borrowed over three thousand dollars from my dad to get started and I was able to pay him back in two weeks. It was the first time he was ever openly proud of me. I started partying then a lot more I guess it was all of the stress but my drinking began to get worse. On top of running the crew I also started a coin shop and I had that to worry about too. A lot of the crew started losing faith in my cause of all of my drinking. I was just depressed I assured them that I will not let them down. Coriee's sister came to work for me and she helped run the female agents I had. Coriee went to Florida with the crew and I stayed behind to run the coin shop.

Two weeks later a girl came in and sold me some gold and she asked me if I was hiring anyone. I knew that Coriee wouldn't be coming back and I was lonely. Her name was Katelyn I hired her and taught her about coins and taught her how to sell them. We hit it off really well but she was dating someone else so we just stayed good friends. We stayed that way for three months and we started getting closer and I'm sure it was because I had money or at least it appeared I did. We also started sleeping together which was one of the biggest mistakes in of my life. My coin shop started doing really good. People in the community were happy for me and I was finally fulfilling one of my dreams of owning my own business an honest one.

Coriee called me one day and told me that the crew was falling apart. I went to help and left Katelyn in charge I thought it would be ok because my dad lived right up the street and could look in from time to time. So I left and drove the van I had to Florida to help Coriee out. When I got there it was a mess everyone was unorganized and running amuck. I wanted to scream and shout at everyone but I was never really one for such things still it took me almost three months to fix everything that she did. I missed my coin shop and because Coriee's and mine relationship was all about business I really didn't want to be around her all that much reminded me about things I would rather have forgotten. But the longer I stayed with her the more I regretted cheating on her I really did love her and I always will.

Well after I helped Coriee get things back in order I flew back to Pittsburgh. I found that Katelyn had been stealing from my store. I had no choice but to fire her. It was hard but I learned a long time ago that you do not mix pleasure with business. I had to close the shop until I could get some extra money. I wanted my dad to run the shop but at the time he was under doctors orders not to work. He had recently had a heart attack and could not work for four months so I had to close the doors for at least that long. I decided to join back up with Coriee I had a feeling things had gotten bad again with the crew.

It turns out I was right she picked me up in Texas where the crew was now. One of the vans broke down and only had two agents. They were barely making enough to pay the rent at the hotels they were staying at. I needed three thousand dollars to fix the van or we would be stuck there in Texas and we needed to get back to California. So I sold my Rolex and got the van fixed. I needed to rebuild the crew so I called an old friend of mine from Boss' crew a kid named Jeff. He agreed and he came and worked for me. He looked all drugged out and he told me he had been taking meth. He told me that he would stop once he started working for me.

He started for me and like he promised he stopped the meth and he was pretty good at making sales. One night he wanted to get some beer so I drove him to a nearby gas station. Jeff forgot his ID so I bought it for him and gave it to him. The next thing I know the police were surrounded the van and said that Jeff was a minor and this was a sting. They had an arrest warrant for Jeff and they took him to jail. I lost a good salesman and at the same time got a ticket for giving a minor alcohol. Fortunately three hours later they let him go and I got my salesman back.

I was able to save up enough money to get my old Lexus sent to me which helped me get around and really helped us rebuild the crew. We took the crew to a casino and we were winning money left and right. We spent the next few days at the casino and right before we left Coriee and I decided to hang out for a day. It was awesome and it was like the good old days. It was close to a perfect day and I could almost forget all of my pain and depression. It was ruined when Jeff called me and told me he wrecked the van arrg will it ever end?

After a massive headache I got the van fixed and I left for San Francisco and I added four more guys for the crew and I was shocked when Coriee found her mother which she hadn't seen since she was a little girl. They ended up being a lot alike and had a lot of fun. It also seemed like she was a good luck charm because the crew took off better than ever. I started drinking a lot more again despite all of our success it seemed like no matter what I did I was still empty and still stuck. I also tried to lose myself in gambling. I wanted to escape so I planned on going home for a while and try and straighten myself up. I saved up three thousand dollars and few back to Pittsburgh and stayed with my dad again.

I was there less than a week when Coriee called me and told me that Jeff got drunk and broke all of the windows in our hotel and stole our van. It was just another bad hand played against me this job was like a curse. I had Coriee report the car stolen and Jeff was pulled over on his way to LA and three thousand dollars later and a trip to jail for Jeff I got my van back so I could get my crew up and running again. I was so sick of California so I sent the crew north to Washington and from there we went to Oregon.

I hired another beautiful girl named Keri and she started selling right away and everything was looking on the up and up finally. Steve started calling me again he wanted us to combine crews and partner up. I went along for a while but he started making a lot off since I talked it over with Coriee and she told me it was up to me. I have always been a pretty forgiving person so I decided to go ahead and give Steve another chance despite everything that had already happened. So Steve set up an appointment with us to discuss our mutual business deal.

I was still a little wary about Steve however but I was in desperate need of money because of the seven thousand dollar ticked I received because of Jeff. Steve made me a deal and said he would buy the van from us for the seven thousand we owe and then went as far as got it fixed as a motion of goodwill. I had four good agents and my star agent named Dustin who was incredible with words and made one heck of a salesman so I still had some say in our agreement. I was also a little nervous of the fact that I was in debt and Steve had millions of dollars from all the years he had been running it and he knew it. I knew I was also partially at his mercy. So our deal was struck and I signed my business over to him and he gave me a four thousand dollar refund. I didn't really have a choice and neither did he I needed him and he needed me.

So Steve and his wife moved into our hotel along with all of their agents. I found myself really proud of Steve he had changed a lot since the last time I saw him. He was calmer and a lot nicer. But I still had mixed feelings. We hired a lot of people but both Dustin and Keri quit because they didn't like Steve. But Steve assured me that he would take care of Coriee and me if anything happened despite them quitting. I was happy when an old roommate and friend of mine named Jack came and joined our new crew which brought in a lot more sales.

Our crew started making tons of money and I started becoming real cocky and stuck up. I let people know I had money and they didn't I didn't care who I hurt or who they were to me they were somehow less. Steve started stressing me out again and called me literally thirty to forty times a day to 'check' in on our crew's progress. Almost all of the crew quit because of the stress and I was left right where I left off. I quit and Coriee was made Steve's manager I was happy for her but I wanted to try and get my old coin company back up and running.

I was able to raise three thousand dollars to help my dad start back up the coin business and keep it going. It was then that a harsh reality hit me. My debts at the time were well over two hundred thousand dollars. I wanted to run away and I did just that I sold the ring I was going to give Coriee I knew it was never going to be and I used that money to get me to Colorado. I was halfway there when I decided to call an old Christian friend of mine named Russ. I broke down and told him everything I was scared and my spirit was broken. He was a Christian Pastor with a family and three beautiful kids but despite that he took me in sensing I needed help or I might not be able to escape the prison I had built for myself. He let me stay in his basement.

I had a lot of Hell on me and I was so lost. I only stayed with Russ for a week but during that time his prayers and support broke some of it off me and gave me some measure of peace. I was able to get eight hundred dollars from my coin shop which was once again becoming successful. I wasn't sure what I was going to do I knew I couldn't stay with Russ his plate was already full and I knew if I went back now I would just be sucked back into my prison. I started going to church and at the end of the week I just packed up and took off for the mountains to get away from it all.

I found a place high in the mountains and a kind old lady let me stay there as long as I helped her paint and do things around the house. I started getting a hold of some old friends from old crews. Still wanted to be in the magazine business but this time I wanted to do it right and be fare with people and stay away from the corrupted nature I was used to. I got back in contact with Leia, Jack, and Jimmy and we started talking. I made them all managers and we started the new crew. The bad part of it is none of us wanted to work we just wanted to party so the start stuttered on for a while. We eventually saved up the money and headed for Tennessee where Leia was from and we went to a nearby hotel. I loved being with Leia again and we were so happy to be back together she had been through Hell and back while she was a porn star and we both still cared about each other.

Well things started getting bad again we were not making any money with this new crew and we had to move to Atlanta and try and start again. This sounds familiar doesn't it? I knew months earlier that if I went back I would be sucked back in. I ignored it deceiving myself that if my intentions were good then it would be ok. I could not be more wrong. The new crew convinced me to stop and get some drugs for them another stupid mistake I didn't really care anymore however cause I was still so happy about being with Leia. The hotel that the crew and I got was the coke capital of the world and I started getting sucked into a bad drug habit. Leia started dancing at a club and I went to watch her one night and made a real bad fool of myself and of her. She and I got in a fight on the way back to the hotel and she got real drugged out and I didn't see her for over a day. I felt as if I was going crazy it felt like there was no end in sight.

I also wanted to add this to the story. Abortions were a common thing on the crew. I really was totally against it. I remember to this day Steve making me take a girl to Planned Parenthood. I told him I did not want to be a part of it. Of course he talked me into it I had a sick feeling when I got back to see him. I told him I would never do that again period. He joked about it and said that OK if another girl gets pregnant we will send them home. The reason Steve wanted them to do it was because he didn't want to lose money. If he sent them home they could not sell anymore. Lord have mercy on your soul Steve!

The reason I stayed in the industry for long was because I was use to the abuse. From my childhood until I got off the road for good its all I knew. See almost everybody that joins comes from a broken family or a abusive background. The ads for the job attract that type of person. The owners and managers know that, so they know how to manipulate you. They use your past to benefit them and control you. That's exactly what Satan does. Very scary! Now the I know the truth! Also if they are not for a bad family they leave with in the first week. Once you are there for 1 year or more it is going to take a act of god for you to get out.

Chapter Four

Highway to the Cross

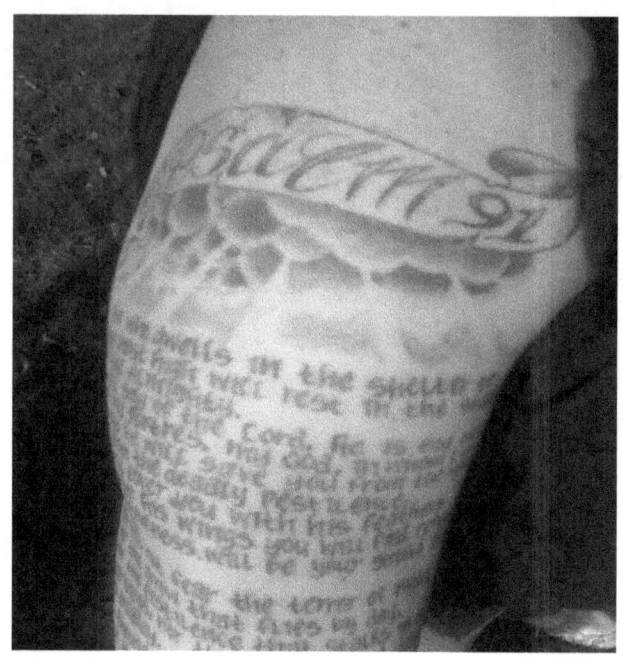

John 8:36; For whom the sin sets free, freed indeed

I knew we had to get out of Atlanta so I took Leia with me and headed for North Carolina. The whole crew was all drugged out and I wanted to get back to Pittsburgh so I could get some help from my dad. Jack came and convinced us to all join up with the Methadone Clinic to go through drug rehab. I convinced Leia to come with me but after just a day she flipped out and left. I later found out that she became a prostitute and a slave for drugs. I was so sad that I cried myself to sleep for weeks.

Leia called me a few weeks later crying saying she was sorry and wanted to go back home and get help. I could barely pay for my rent so I left to go to her. Leia's parents were very inviting and let me stay there with them and Leia. I stayed with them for a while and I started becoming very sick and Leia's parents took care of me. After I recovered her dad lent us five hundred dollars and we left for Florida so I could start another crew.

She got a job as a dancer again and within a week she was on so many drugs she could hardly think straight. She started staying out really late and told me she was working but she had little money to back that up. I knew then that this was not going to work out. I was also really trying to live right again and started reading the bible every day and I began to realize that everything I was doing was going against everything in it. My beliefs were about to clash with my life. I dropped off Leia off at work one last time and I packed up my things and called up Jack. I told him what was happening and he was able to wire me two hundred bucks for gas and told me to go to him in Miami. On the way there something told me to call up a very old friend of mine from my first crew, a guy named Joe.

I called him at like two in the morning when he didn't answer the first time something told me to call him a second time. He answered then and I told him everything. Joe had since cleaned up his life and was now going to school to become a minister. He said I could come and stay with him as long as I needed to. I felt like I was supposed to stay with him so I packed up my things and moved in. I called my dad and let him know where I was and told him I was safe and finally ready to really change my life around.

Joe and I started praying together and reading the bible together every day. I begged God to save me and change my heart. It was hard for me to say the least I had done so much and I felt as if I could never be set free or deserved to be forgiven from the things I had done. I know now that sometimes in order to receive freedom you must first hit rock bottom which God was about to do.

I called my dad and told him I was ok and I started reading the bible every day. I had always wanted to sent my life straight and get right with God but it wasn't until now that I started seeing how. Joe taught me a lot about God. I related very well with Joe because he had served on the crew same as I did and made a lot of the same mistakes that I did. It gave me hope.

We started an internet business together and I started selling advertising for Christian magazines. Things looked as if my life were about to turn around until I hooked up with a land lord named Kenny who I was going to rent from to move my coin business to Graceville where I was now staying. It was fine until I got drunk with him and Joe kicked me out he said that he couldn't have alcohol or drugs in his house so I was left once again with nothing. And the lady I worked for fired me because of it. I felt like God had abandoned me and I fell back off the wagon as it were.

I had no home no job and didn't have any way to get back home. I became really depressed and I started to drown myself in bars once again trying to run from my problems. I met old guy in a bar and he asked if I could give him a ride home. I had y truck at the time the last real possession I had left. I don't normally give rides to strangers but I was lonely and wanted to talk to someone so I took him home.

I told him about my problems and he said I could stay with him. He was like fifty or sixty a big biker dude but he still seemed like an ok guy. He said that for a hundred bucks a moth he would let me stay with him until I got back on my feet he then said that once I had a job however the rent would be three hundred. So I paid the man the hundred for the first month and crashed at his place. Within a day we ran out of beers so the guy took me to a bar that was straight out of hell. It was the creepiest place I had ever seen in my life.

The bar tender looked like the living dead and there was a freaky woman there with a wooden leg. But she was nice, I drank just as much out of fear as I did to cover my pain. We both got so drunk we couldn't contain ourselves and we started fighting. I'm not even sure about what I can't remember. Anyway the bartender said we had to leave and the biker dude tried to drag me out of the bar and the woman with the wooden leg helped me and told me to leave. God Bless that woman. On top of that the old man took off in my truck. I was so drunk I didn't care at the moment. I called a cab and gave him the last of my money and he took me to a hotel.

I had previously paid for a month's worth of rent at

this hotel and I had a few days left before it wasn't paid for any longer; so I went to my room and slept for two days. I woke up in a daze I was wondering what happened and where my truck was. I was about to call the cops until I remembered that the old man had taken it.

I couldn't remember where he lived but I did remember where that bar was and I went their asking about the old man. They told me where he was and I went back to his house. When I knocked on the door he said that everything was cool and he apologized for taking my truck. I just wanted it back so I took the keys and left. To this day that bar and that night was the scarcest place I have ever been to and I sincerely believe that that bar was straight out of Hell.

I was so depressed I went back to the hotel I had only forty dollars left and I wanted to end it all. I just wanted to jump off the balcony and end the pain and everything. I turned on the T.V. it was on TBN and it just happened to be about suicide prevention and help. They offered to help anyone who was having suicidal thought and the like. Even though I wanted to end it I was afraid to so I called them up and asked for help.

They told me to get to a hospital they found one about forty five minutes away. I checked in and stayed for about ten days. They gave me the help and medicine I needed and I was completely honest with them about everything. They found a mission for me in Alabama and sent me to live there for a while. I also called up my dad and told him everything that had happened. My dad wanted me to come back home but I didn't. Instead I called up Steve he was in Houston. I had only stayed at the mission for ten days and it helped a lot but I was behind on bills and I needed the job and had no choice. Or so I thought.

I barely had enough gas to get to Kenny's house and I sold him an old shoe box buffer and buffed all of his shoes. It earned me seventy bucks. Steve was in Huston and that was where I was going I ran out of gas and money halfway there. Coincidently I ran out at a gas station but I had no money for gas. I met an old man there and I asked him if I could borrow a few bucks for gas he asked me what was wrong and I told him everything. He just nodded and filled up my tank God bless that man!

Well I made it to Houston six thirty on a Sunday morning the guys I was going to meet their about the job were not answering their phones. I heard that Joel Osteen's church was nearby so I decided to pop in. I had always wanted to go to that church just to see what the service was like. That happened to be the best thing I had ever done for myself. I walked in and some people took me to the front of the church I couldn't believe what happened next. God hit me like a ton of bricks with his love. He touched the deepest part of my heart and soul and set me free completely. I knew then that there really was a God! I started working for the Magazine Crews again after that but it only lasted a few weeks I could not take it anymore and I quit the magazine business for good. I would no longer be a slave to the Sale to the Money or to the Power that I had given myself over to.

I had just enough money to get back home it was and I went straight to my brother's house, he welcomed me with open arms. Within two weeks I closed down my old coin shop which had caused a bad headache for my father I sold the rest of my coins to pay off all my bills. I had so much peace. I could not believe the weight that had lifted off me with the reality of not having to travel or stay in my prison. My lifelong nightmare had ended and now I was completely free at long last.

Chapter Five

Aftermath

John 3:16; For God so loved the world that he gave His only begotten son that whosoever believes in him shall not die but have eternal life.

After I moved out of my brother house, I still had a wondering spirit and was praying. I disparately needed fellowship with other Christian but I was scared. My shame plagued me. I was taking anti depression medication it was messing me up. I wrote most of the book when I was depressed. I was having vivid dreams of being in hell and back on the road. Sleeping too much and not being able to sleep. Knowing that god was still working on me I pressed on.

I found a church in walking distance from his house. It was an Assembly of God church. I got to the church at 9:30am and could not wait for the church doors to open. I was sitting outside the doors waiting. The pastor walked up to me on the way in and said praise god good to have you today. He said I'm Pastor Mike he looked like Samuel L Jackson and kind of spoke like him to. I new I found a good church and felt god's presence instantly.

It has been awhile since I went to church but I know that's the biggest part of being a Christian. We must gather together for god's will to be more affective. My friend Russ always told me to go to church and get around other

Christians. I finally was moving in the direction god wanted me to. I felt a big burden come off of me after the service and Pastor Mike had went through some of the things I did in life with drugs. I related to him I really look up to him.

After church I went back to my brother's and was hanging out with my niece Samatha and it made me think. I have been gone for so long and I missed a lot of her life. I began to feel guilty but joyful at the same time. I missed her so much and now have a new reason to live. She is ten now and a beautiful child. My family and me have never really bounded, god was about to fix it all. He is good at that when you stay in the word and do his will.

About 2 months pass, all I did was go to bible studies and worked on this book, it was on my heart to get this story out there.

One day coming home from a bible study I got a call from an old friend. He worked for Bob and then Todd. So he knew kind of what I went through. He asked me if a wanted to met with him, I was a little scared but said OK. About two days pass and he picked me up. He took me out to dinner with his wife and asked me if I wanted a job. I quickly said yes. God is awesome! After living with my brother for two months it was time for me to get on with my life.

Two days go by and then I picked up and left. I found a little apartment close to the new job. It was crazy there was only one car in the parking lot of this large complex. I decided to stop and did not have a lot of money to pay for hotels. I was sick of hotels anyway. Outside there was a phone number so a called it. The next thing I knew I guy came out and show the apartment to me. It was a mess and filthy, but I didn't have a lot of options. I ask if he would take $350 for the first month and I will clean it up. He agreed. So I moved in! God showed up again! After cleaning the place it starting looking nice and was the first place I could finally call home.

My friend showed and told me I needed a driver licensee to get the job but I have. Well I had some issues in Florida and needed about $200 to fix my problem and my birth certificate. God showed up again, my friend paid them off for me and took me to get my birth certificate. The bad thing was it was going to take about a month for the process of the renewal. I needed to start working fast to cover my rent.

The next day I seen that the other apartments in the building were vacant and seen an opportunity. I call the landlord and ask her if I fixed up the remaining 4 units and rent them. Then I asked her if she would help me out. God showed up again! She said yes! My next months rent was covered.

My brother needed a new place because things were not working out for him with his wife they fought way too much and they needed a brake. So he came out and rented 1 on the units. Then I put an ad up on Craigslist to rent the remaining apartments. The next day a guy named Dan emailed me about a place. I met with him and he told me he was a Christian. I said when can you move in. He said about a month. Not knowing that god was about to move my relationship with him to the next level.

That month goes by, the first guy I met here his name is Don he's the one that showed me the apartment. While come to find out Don is the mayor of the town, I never had a clue. We became good friends and he would drive me around to get supplies and take me out to dinner. What a great friend to have. I told him about my life and he really accepted me. I looked up to him as a father figure as soon as a met him. In the bible it says to seek wise counsel. I finally found it!

Dan finally moves in and the other two apartments finally become occupied. The landlord was happy with me. I started my new job and they gave me a car to drive. God is awesome! The job is long hours but any work is good work for me after all I have been through. I started making good money and after I was there for 90 days I got health insurance. God showed up again! I needed it because I had to get my wisdom teeth out and have been in pain for about a year. So after the 90 days I had the operation and it was painful after words. I could not go back to work for about a month. Once again not able to pay my rent.

After the operation I started healing but was in so much pain. I was on pain medication it reminded me of my addictions. So one day I threw the rest of it down the toilet and told myself I will deal with the pain. Don my neighbor took me the hospital the next night and I got non addictive medication and some antibiotics. With in days I was feeling better but the dreams from the road came back.

One day I was playing basketball outside the units and Dan drove up. He asked me if I wanted to go to dinner with him. I said sure, at dinner I began telling him of my ordeal and my life. He welcomed me to go to church with him on Sunday of course I said yes. When we got back he handed me $300 I could not believe it. He said god told him to give it to me. Wow! God showed up again! After that I paid my rent and the next day he asked if I wanted to go to a men's conference in Baltimore for his church. It was for 3 days I was unsure what to expect but I quickly said yes!

We got there and met up with others from his old church they were very welcoming. We drove the rest of the way and when we got there checked into a hotel. Staying in a hotel again brought back bad memories. I could not sleep at all. The services were awesome no matter how tired I was. There were 5 altar calls all of them had my name on them. I ran down for everyone and the presence of god was all over me. I was finally in a place were I thought I should be, I never felt some much peace in my whole life.

When we got back we attended church the next morning I felt the best I have ever felt in a long time. After the service I was so thankful for Dan he was the angel god sent to me. Since then my relationships with my family are the best it's ever been. I have been attending church regularly. This Thanksgiving and Christmas is the first one

I will share with them in over 20 years.

I got my soul back and god's love. For all the people that do not believe in god all I have to say is "JESUS" he made me free. Stay in the word of god. Meditate on the verses daily. Find a bible-based spirit-filled church. Tithe 10% of your first earnings to the lord's work. Put god first he will take you places you had never been. "PRAISE AND GLORY TO OUR LORD AND SAVIOR JESUS"

The book needed editing and probably still does. All the editing was done by a Christian kid named Chris I met in the last my travels. He is a miracle that god give me. Without him this book could not have happened. When I started this project I was bitter and just wanted to tell my story. He made me realize god's grace and the truth what set me free.

I am now finally rebuilding relationships with my

friends and family. I have done my share of long-suffering and am now finding favor in the sight of the Lord. I dedicate this book to Jesus Christ my Lord and Savior to whom I owe my life and my family. I have learned that it is indeed easier for a camel to pass through the eye of a needle than it is a rich man to enter the kingdom of heaven. And that God so loved the world he gave his own begotten son that who so ever believes in him will not die.

I know that with Christ I am free and only through him am it possible. I am forgiven and I am alive as I never have been before. God bless you guy's thanks for hearing my story.

I am now at peace knowing that I have been forgiven and set free. It is all because of Jesus that this happened and I am convinced it is the only way to be completely free. The change in my life has also changed that of my father's and brother's life as well. Remember God loves you and he doesn't want you to live in a living hell. He is willing and able to set you free if you will allow him to. I continue to read the word daily it has been the only thing that has really added to my life and has helped me understand who God is and who I was and am meant to be.

I hope and pray that this book will bring freedom and warning to others who have lived or are living in the same type of prison I was living in. Like it says in the bible a traveler will end with nothing! I am so glad to have made it back at long last. I love my family very much and until now I had not realized how much I missed them all. I have found God! The best decision I ever made in my life.

**Thanks to all of the people that helped me get my quota
God bless you!**

Who The Son Has Set Free _Is_ Free Indeed!

I would like to end this chapter with a scripture I had read every night throughout my ordeals and has meant a lot to me ever since I joined the magazine crews. I would read and pray Psalms 91 sometimes at night from the bible that is kept in every hotel I have been to and it helped guide my way ever since...

PSALMS 91

"He who dwells within the secrete place of the most high shall abide under the shadow of the almighty. I will say of the lord "he is my fortress; my god; in him I will trust."

Surely he will deliver you from the snares of the enemy. He shall cover you with his feathers, and under his wings you shall take refuge, his truth shall be your shield and buckler. You shall not be afraid of the terror by night, nor the arrow that flies by day, nor the pestilence that walked in the darkness. Nor the destruction that lays waist at noonday.

A thousand may fall at you side. And ten thousand by your right hand; but it shall not come near you. Only with your eyes will you look and see the reward of the wicked. Because you have made the lord your fortress. Even the most high you're your dwelling place.

No evil shall befall you, nor shall any plague come near your dwelling; for he shall give his angles charge over you. In their hands they shall bear you up. Lest you dash your foot upon the stone. You shall tread upon the lion and the cobra the young lion and the serpent you shall trample underfoot.

Because he has set his love upon me, therefore I will deliver him; I will set him on high because he has known my name. He shall call upon me and I shall answer him; I will be with him in trouble I will deliver him and honor him. With long life I will satisfy him, and show him my salvation.

TAM-A-GBY !
Thanks a Million and God bless you

Chapter 6

Dangers of Taking the Job

Timothy 3:1-3:4 this is know also, that in the last days perilous times shall come. For men shall be lovers of their own selves, covetous, boasters, proud, blasphemers, disobedient to parents, unthankful, unholy. Without natural affection, trucebreakers, false accusers, incontinent, fierce, despisers of those that are good. Traitors, heady, high-minded, lovers of pleasures more than lovers of god.

12 DANGERS OF TAKING THE JOB

1. The company will issue a 1099 to you and reports all your earnings, housing costs, and misc. costs to the IRS which means you are will end up owing the government money. You will have to pay back sooner than later.

2. There is no health or medical benefits, so if you get sick you will end up with unpaid medical bills. They will still make you work even if you are deathly ill.

3. You will sign an independent contractor's agreement. The contract states that the company is not liable for any actions by other crew's members, customers and management.

4. Allot of companies do not do background checks, but claim to do so. So you really do not know who you are

working or rooming with.

5. There is a lot of reckless driving, unsafe vans, un-licensed drivers and sometimes the companies do not register or have insurance on the vans. You will spend at 80% of your career traveling in these vans.

6. There is no 401k/Pension so if you decided to make a career out of it. You will leave with what you started with nothing but unpaid tickets, fines, taxes and debt.

7. You will be staying in hotel / motels that normally have allot of shady people staying at. Drug dealers, thieves, and hookers are most of the time present. Most of the time the hotels are in the worst neighborhoods in the cities you stay in. The company can only get cheap rates in those places. You will room with up to four others in one little room.

8. You will be dropped off by yourself most of the time to

work ten to twelve hour days. The neighborhoods and shopping centers you will be selling in are all over the country in which there are allot of dangerous people you may or may not come into contact with. Since the company only hires young adults eight-teen to twenty-three years of age. The girls have the most problems for obvious reasons.

9. The police will harass you, issue you tickets and some times arrest you for soliciting without a permit. The company never registers to get them. When you get in trouble, most of the time they will not help you.

10. When you are not selling you will be verbally abused by other crew members and there is a possibility of physical abuse as well. The managers or owners are the worst allot of them are worst then the crew members.

11. The owners and managers will lie and say they care about your well being. Really all they care about is their own personal greed.

12. "I WANT TO GO HOME" If you want to leave, most of the time they will not pay for your return trip or try to talk you into staying. Voice your opinion on the way out or cause them any grief at all. They and or other crew members might even get violent.

I wrote this chapter for the nice lady that runs www.magcrew.com a website that helping others in and out of the door to door magazine sales business. Go to this website for more information about the magazine business.

Chapter 7

The History of the Business

Mathew 7:7-7:8 Ask, and it shall be given to you; seek, and ye shall find; knock, and it shall be opened unto you.

Articles I found relating to the door to door magazine and other similar businesses. Writers are unknown or deceased. The door to door business was once an honest and respectful business. That changed through out history for the worse. Hope this will bring some light into now a dark industry.

For as long as I can remember, I've wondered why every newspaper, magazine, and news cast contains only negative content. Think about it. No matter what you read, see or hear under the guise of NEWS, 99.9% of it refers to murder, death, crime, war, disease, scandal, etc. I've heard the universal answer many times: "Good news doesn't sell. People simply aren't interested in good news." However, I've always doubted that observation and held out a little hope that others enjoyed good news as much as I did.

When I was a youngster, about 100 years ago, you could buy a colorful comic book for a mere 10¢. Today they cost anywhere from three to four dollars each. Almost every comic book contained want ads offering anything from ant farms and sea monkeys to job opportunities in the form of Christmas card sales and paper routes.

One of those ads resulted in my first "real job" other than mowing lawns at the ripe old age of 8. I considered myself a newspaper man of sorts by signing up to deliver a weekly newspaper door to door. I had to recruit my own customers from scratch using a sales pitch I developed myself. Little did I know at the time that I was one of approximately 30,000 boys collecting dimes from more than 700,000 American small town homes from coast to coast? I made 5¢ on every copy I sold, won a variety of "swell" prizes and built my route to include well over a hundred customers and several commercial partners who resold my papers in their establishment. I had no idea that what I thought was a little weekly newspaper was actually a national institution.

Grit's early history including the news-carrier program, which for decades had newsboys selling Grit door-to-door and on street corners.

This was their ad to recruit young adult's looks familiar!

Forty years ago, a knock on the front door during the day was not all that unusual. Far more women worked in the home then than now, and companies had sales forces that went door-to-door, showing their products and making sales to this sizeable market.

Perhaps the most successful was the Fuller Brush Company. Alfred C. Fuller (1885-1973), born in Nova Scotia, came to Boston as a young man, hoping to make his fortune. In 1905 he found work with the Somerville Brush and Mop Company, which had been started by one of his brothers. Alfred discovered that he had a "gift" for sales and that he could gain the confidence of housewives by demonstrating the various brushes in their homes. He also found that they often had ideas for improving the product.

The following year, Fuller, together with a sister, started his own company in the basement of her home. Fuller would go door-to-door during the day, demonstrate his wares, take orders and deposits, and then return home to make the brushes, which he would then deliver. The products actually were sold before they were made, a novel and cost-efficient system.

Fuller found that his business was growing too large for a one-person operation, and he began to recruit a sales force. Fuller representatives had to purchase their own sample case, stocked with products, and were assigned a territory. The charismatic Fuller offered training and tips, but had difficulty finding the right type of person. In 1909 he began advertising in magazines for salesmen. The investment paid off, and by 1910 he had 260 dealers.

Fuller emphasized positive thinking and developed a sales structure that promoted supervisors from the ranks of successful salesmen. By 1910 annual sales amounted to more than $1 million. That figure grew to $15 million by 1923.

In 1921 the Saturday Evening Post magazine coined the term "Fuller Brush Man," and it quickly became a part of the language. Like Henry Ford and Thomas Edison, Fuller became a folk hero who had risen from humble beginnings to become a self-made millionaire.

In the later 1920s, Fuller's sales fell, primarily because he had difficulty getting salesmen. The Great Depression, which began in 1929, actually saw an increase in business. By the outbreak of World War II, sales had returned to previous levels. During the war, the company produced for the military.

Post-World War II prosperity saw the company continue to expand. Fuller Brush had become such an institution that two movies - The Fuller Brush Man (1948) and The Fuller Brush Girl (1950) - placed lead actors Red Skelton and Lucille Ball in the role of Fuller salespeople.

But times were changing. Many wives began to work outside of the home. Television advertising and shopping centers were on the rise. Companies that relied upon door-to-door sales, including Fuller, suffered. All too often, the knock on the door was not answered.

An even more spectacular story of door-to-door selling success is the case of Forest S. Barrett. In 1941, when direct, salesmanship was still only a mild ripple in selling American products; he took a job with a Bible distribution firm! He went from door to door using this sales pitch: "Read the Bible to be wise. Believe it to be safe. And practice it to be holy."

In a few years, he became the firm's sales manager. Then he accepted a partnership in the company. By 1945, the company was changed to Barrett Distributors and moved to Dallas, Texas Forest S. Barrett, president and sole owner. He is now backed by a force of 300 door-to-door salesmen and an office staff of 30 employees. His estimated sales for 1951 were close to $3,000,000.

In fact, Barrett added a new twist to launching door-to-door salesmen on the road to self-employment. He used the chain-letter principle, calling it pyramiding partnership. He formed a partnership agreement with a salesman and left that salesman free to form a similar (or different) profit agreement with anyone else. Each succeeding salesman, thereafter, joined the previous salesman in a separate agreement of his own. Today, Barrett claims "anyone capable of following instructions, recruiting, hiring and managing other people" has unlimited opportunities with him.

Of course, there's nothing new under the sun and door-to-door selling is no exception. Experts trace it back to the first itinerant peddlers a couple of thousand years ago. However, as a big business, the history of door-to-door selling is comparatively recent. In 1852, C. W. Stuart and Co. of Newark, N. Y. started selling trees and shrubs directly to the consumer instead of through the established channels. Then, in 1868 a man named J. R. Watkins bought a small bottle of liniment from a doctor who made his own preparation. Watkins soon found the liniment popular with his own friends. On an impulse, he decided it could be sold more widely if it were brought directly to the attention of the housewife. Introducing what was also probably the first free-trial offer, Watkins went around in an enclosed wagon, leaving a few bottles at each house. When he made a second call, those who liked the liniment paid; those who didn't returned the unused portion.

Today, the J. R. Watkins Co. of Winona, Minn, sells hundreds of items and employs more than 15,000 door-to-door salesmen who ring up $45,000,000 worth of business annually. They serve some 20,000,000 customers.

But it took two brothers, Clarence E. Knapp and Elwin Knapp, right after World War I, to prove that you can sell almost anything by ringing doorbells. Looking around for new business ideas, they chose the shoe industry. But their decision was revolutionary for they decided to sell directly to the customer with a product that businessmen swore couldn't be sold outside a retail store. They opened a small factory in Brockton, Mass. Then Clarence scooted out to Chicago to open an office, advertising for door-to-door salesmen. Hundreds flocked to his hotel room for interviews. Nearly all left just as fast as they came when they saw that it was shoes they would have to sell. One man stayed behind.

He was curious enough to ask: "How can you sell shoes without a store where you can invite a man to be properly fitted?"

"Come," said Clarence Knapp, "I'll show you." And he took him over to a group of newspaper truck drivers cluttered around the Chicago Daily News building waiting to haul away the latest edition.

Within a couple of hours, Clarence sold 19 pairs of shoes from a suitcase. Today, the man who was with him supervises dozens of door-to-door salesmen from his slick Chicago office. And the name of Knapp Bros. Shoe Manufacturing Co. hangs over three factories producing men's shoes at capacity. Recently, Knapp Bros, door-to-door salesmen sold more shoes in one month than in any similar period in its entire history. And every pair is still sold without benefit of a store.

Nowadays, if you want to set yourself up as an independent door-to-door salesman, working as little or as long as you like each day, the list of things you can sign up to sell is practically endless, automatic floor waxes, pop-corn machines, brushes, vacuum cleaners, pots and pans, tools, gas and oil savers, fruit trees, machine tools, ball point pens, greeting cards, food products, insecticides, soap, razor blades, fire extinguishers, store signs, radios, typewriters and even magazines. In a tough, competitive market like New York, for instance, it was estimated recently that about 50 per cent of all the television sets sold in the area were sold by direct salesmen.

Of course, door-to-door selling today does not mean that you have to restrict your efforts to the housewife. The big trend is toward specialization. Many door-to-door salesmen sell only to people who run institutions. Many just visit garage owners. Some call on offices, others on private homes only. Most manufacturers who supply products for door-to-door selling don't care where you're from or even where you're going to sell. They only want to be sure that you're not too bashful to carry their products directly to potential customers.

Like any other business, door-to-door selling has its share of unscrupulous characters. Not so long ago, several door-to-door salesmen got housewives to open doors for them by pretending they were taking a survey. Once inside the door, the salesman would ask a few innocent questions on a dummy form, then he would proceed to sell his own products. You can imagine how much this angered housewives.

Recent war talk has even made it possible for some salesmen to capitalize on the gullibility of people. One such salesman was arrested last year in Los Angeles for selling "anti-atom-bomb" lotion. It turned out to be nothing more than a smooth, homemade mixture of water and cold cream, for which he was getting $2.49 for half a pint. It cost him six cents to make.

Other unscrupulous salesmen talked people into buying special clothing for protection against the effects of an atomic explosion. Such clothing, of course, doesn't exist.

Up to a housewife's door in Alexandria, La. one day in 1949 stepped Magazine Salesman Jack H. Beard to sell combination subscriptions to several magazines (Saturday Evening Post, Newsweek and Ladies Home Journal). But Beard was really trying to get arrested, to test a city ordinance forbidding door-to-door visits without prior permission of householders. Obligingly, Alexandria's police arrested Salesman Beard, and he was ordered to pay a $25 fine or go to jail for 30 days.

Three associations, representing door-to-door sellers of everything from Fuller Brushes to encyclopedias, joined with Beard to appeal his case, since the law dealt a heavy blow to the house-to-house selling of $1.4 billion in consumer goods each year, including some 10,000,000 magazine subscriptions. They wanted to test the constitutionality of the "Green River" ordinance which over 400 U.S. communities have adopted since Green River, Wyo. passed the first one in 1931 to slam the door on solicitors. Beard's lawyers charged that his arrest violated both freedom of the press and free speech. Last week, by 6-to-3, the U.S. Supreme Court ruled otherwise, affirmed the right of any community to restrict door-to-door selling. Justice Stanley Reed, speaking for the majority, wrote: "Subscriptions may be made by anyone interested in receiving the magazines without the annoyances of house-to-house canvassing."

The name Green River Ordinance is given to a common American city ordinance prohibiting door-to-door solicitation. Under such an ordinance, it is illegal for any business to sell their items door-to-door without express permission from the household beforehand. Some versions prohibit all organizations, including non-profit charitable, political, and religious groups, from soliciting or canvassing any household that makes it clear, in writing, that it does not want such solicitations (generally with a "No Trespassing" or "No Solicitations" sign posted.)

The ordinance is named for the city of Green River, Wyoming, the first city to enact it.

The ordinance has been brought before the Supreme Court for challenge in several times. While the court has upheld these ordinances when they prohibit intrastate commerce (seeing the issue as a state's rights issue), more recent decisions suggest that a total ban on door to door soliciting would be found unconstitutional and unenforceable on the grounds of religious free speech and commercial free speech when the ordinances ban religious or interstate solicitations.

It has all changed since the nice polite salesman came to your door with a True Grit or a Fuller Brush. Now you really do not know what you are supporting. When someone comes knocking. It's your decision to say "YES" or "NO". I am no longer a door to door salesman. I found there are other door to door businesses still out there that are honest and respectful.

God Bless you all! Keep the lord close to your Heart. I promise it is the best decision you will ever make in your life. He will never leave you or forsake you.

George C. Valentine

www.ingramcontent.com/pod-product-compliance
Lightning Source LLC
Chambersburg PA
CBHW072135280526
45788CB00002B/650